W9-CBE-833

FLOWERS
FOR ALL SEASONS
WINTER

Also by Jane Packer

Celebrating with Flowers
Flowers for all Seasons: Spring
Flowers for all Seasons: Summer
Flowers for all Seasons: Fall

FLOWERS
FOR ALL SEASONS
WINTER

Text by Jane Packer and Elizabeth Wilhide

Fawcett Columbine · New York

A Fawcett Columbine Book
Published by Ballantine Books

Published in Great Britain by Pavilion Books Limited.

Library of Congress Cataloging-in-Publication Data

Packer, Jane. 1959-
    Flowers for all seasons. Winter/text by Jane Packer and
Elizabeth Wilhide.—1st American ed.
        p.   cm.
    Includes index.
    ISBN 0-449-90414-8
    1. Flower arrangement. 2. Flowers. 3. Winter. I. Wilhide.
Elizabeth. II. Title. III. Title: Fall.
SB449.P225 1989
745.92—dc20   88-92871
                                                        CIP

Printed and bound in Spain by Cayfosa Industria Grafica

First American Edition: November 1989

10 9 8 7 6 5 4 3 2 1

Contents

Introduction   7

Winter Flowers and Foliage   8

The Winter Palette   12

A Style for Winter   22

Winter Weddings   54

Special Occasions   72

Basic Techniques   98

Index   110

Acknowledgements   111

Introduction

Winter might well seem an unlikely time to adopt a seasonal approach to flowers and flower arranging. After all, there are hardly any flowers growing in the garden and many florists are only able to supply commercially cultivated varieties grown elsewhere or brought on early.

Nevertheless at the heart of the season there are strong links with nature and the outside world. As the days grow shorter and darker, everything builds towards the Christmas and New Year festivities, a family celebration which is traditionally marked by many kinds of decoration, of which the best known and loved is the Christmas tree. Wreaths, garlands and branches of greenery all have powerful associations with the festive season, associations which predate Christianity and have their origins in the pagan rituals of the winter solstice.

While fresh green boughs, rich red berries, fruits, gold and glitter bring warmth and vitality to the dull days of midwinter, there is another way to express the seasonal mood. This is to recreate the cold, sparse, moody look of the landscape using bare twigs, lichen, a few delicate flowers and muted touches of colour. Dried flowers also provide an invaluable supplement to the seasonal range, more evocative and appropriate than imports.

Once the year has turned the corner and the days are lengthening again, early spring flowers and bulbs bring a promise of warmer weather. The first narcissi are now part of the Christmas scene; hyacinths, daffodils and snowdrops mark the transition from winter to spring.

At first unpromising, winter can provide a rich store of traditions, materials and ideas to give flower arrangements a seasonal emphasis. When the outside world is inhospitable, floral decorations take on a particular importance, making the home more inviting and acting as a reminder that better days are on the way.

JANE PACKER

7

Winter Flowers and Foliage

Whatever flowers manage to keep growing during the winter months will be highly prized and most definitely not for picking. Instead, in the windswept and bedraggled garden, evergreens come into their own, standing out as the only bit of fresh green in a landscape of bare branches and fallen leaves.

Although the garden cannot supply fresh flowers for the home, there are many other ingredients which are useful as part of the winter range, such as moss, ivy, lichen, pine cones, chestnuts, clusters of berries, twigs, holly and fir branches. Many of these can be collected from neglected patches of land, woodland walks, and the like, without harming the environment.

For fresh flowers, however, you will have to rely on what the florist has in stock. At this time of year, in addition to year-round standards, the first bulb flowers will be making an appearance, either potted or cut. In addition, dried flowers extend the possibilities for display.

Much winter colour comes in the form of berries. In this context it is crucial to remember that many berries are poisonous, potentially causing anything from an unpleasant bout of sickness to death. Please do check that you are not bringing an unnecessary risk into the home.

SELECTING FLOWERS

Buying in bud is advisable for most flowers but avoid tight green buds which may never open and opt for those just beginning to show colour.

Always check any flowers wrapped in plastic for signs of botrytis or mildew. Flowers which have been kept wrapped for several days will sweat because of the lack of ventilation and stems and foliage will begin to rot. This can be a particular problem in winter if the flowers have been packed while they were wet.

Right: Rich red roses and a matching candle bring seasonal cheer to a windowsill. Vines are used to bind driftwood in place. Moss and ivy give background depth.

In rainy weather, check that the flowers have not been left standing for hours outdoors.

SOURCES

A good florist is the best source for healthy fresh flowers and will stock a wider range of colours and varieties than the average market stall or corner shop. Shops which only carry flowers as a sideline – petrol stations, for example – may be less reliable, often displaying flowers when they are past their best.

Florists' flowers used to be synonymous with highly cultivated hothouse blooms, to the extent that when "garden" flowers became more commonly available in shops, people showed a certain reluctance to buy them. With fashion now swinging away from the formal and exotic in favour of natural effects, there is less of a distinction between what you can see growing in a garden and what is on sale in a flower shop. The biggest difference is that many flowers appear much earlier in the flower shops than they do in the garden, by virtue of the flowers being commercially cultivated or flown in from warmer areas. And, of course, florists can supply many types of flower virtually all year round.

Planning and planting a garden to create a source of cut flowers for the home is a subject in itself. But unless beds and borders are overflowing with blooms, most people have to compromise between having colour indoors or out. In the winter, there are likely to be so few flowers growing in the garden that picking them for indoor arrangements is not a practical proposition. Instead, concentrate on collecting chestnuts, moss, lichen and interesting vines. Even when devoid of foliage, honeysuckle, for example, can be intriguingly knotted and twisted.

Left: A blaze of colour in a winter hearth has been created by combining red spray roses and red arums with a variety of foliage – eucalyptus, berried ivy, camellia leaves and lichen-covered branches.

Hedgerows, verges and neglected patches of land can also provide plentiful sources of foliage and of trailing stems such as ivy. Remember, however, that wild flowers should never be picked. Areas of true woodland, wild meadows and hedgerows are fast declining, with the loss of many species and it is important to leave the flowers and plants untouched to aid their conservation.

The Winter Palette

ALSTROEMERIA (Peruvian lily; *Alstroemeria* hybrid)
Availability Year-round; cut
Price Medium
Colour range White, pink, red, purple, orange
Life span Very long-lasting
Delicate-looking flower resembling an orchid, but nevertheless very hardy and affordable. Buds will continue to open as main flowers die. There are three to five flower bracts at the top of a long, slender stem. Good for arrangements or wired in wedding bouquets.

AMARYLLIS (*Hippeastrum* hybrids)
Availability October to May; cut or potted
Price Expensive
Colour range White, pink, apricot, red
Life span Very long-lasting
Several buds at top of long tubular foliage-free stem. Large trumpet-like flower. Good used singly in clear glass vases for modern effect, cut low in bowls or wired in wedding bouquets (only use the flower).

ANEMONE (*Anemone coronaria*)
Availability September to May; cut
Price Cheap to medium
Colour range White, pink, red, purple, blue
Life span Long-lasting
Intensely coloured, with velvety petals. Short, mixed bunches are cheap; longer-stemmed varieties cost more. Creates a cottage garden look in simple vases. Can be wired in bouquets if used with care – flowers wilt quickly out of water.

AZALEA (*Rhododendron simsii*)
Availability December to March; cut or potted
Price Medium
Colour range White, pink, purple, red
Life span Long-lasting if cut
Delicate-looking flower surrounded by dark green leaves. Buy potted and cut branches to use in arrangements or wired wedding bouquets. Azaleas wilt dramatically when they are in need of water and can be revived by a good soaking, although leaves will remain flaccid.

BOUVARDIA (*Bouvardia* spp.)
Availability Year-round; cut
Price Expensive
Colour range White, pink, red
Life span Short
Tiny, delicate florets clustered at the top of stem. Prone to wilting and vulnerable to draughts. Best used in a vase rather than oasis arrangements.

BOX (*Buxus sempervirens*)
Availability Year-round; cut
Price Cheap
Colour range Dark green foliage, or variegated yellow and green
Life span Very long-lasting
Tiny, heavy dark green leaves densely massed along branches. Branches are strong, so suitable for large arrangements and for creating topiary shapes.

CARNATION (*Dianthus* sp.)
Availability Year-round; cut
Price Cheap
Colour range White, pink, cream, red, peach, orange, purple
Life span Very long-lasting
Popular and readily recognized flower. Slight perfume, good colour range and longevity but reminiscent of old-fashioned formal arrangements. Shatter large blooms to use segments in wired bouquets.

CHRISTMAS ROSE (*Helleborus niger*)
Availability December to March; cut
Price Expensive
Colour range White
Life span Long-lasting
Traditional Christmas flower, often seen on Christmas card designs but not easy to obtain. White, waxy petals with beautiful green veining, on thick, fleshy short stem. Stunning for Christmas bride.

CHRYSANTHEMUM (*Chrysanthemum* hybrids)
Availability Year-round; cut or potted
Price Cheap to medium
Colour range White, cream, apricot, bronze, pink, red, purple
Life span Very long-lasting
Many different flower varieties, including single, double and "spider" blooms, as well as sprays. I prefer the single chrysanthemum with its cottagey, daisy-like appearance.

CROCUS (*Crocus* hybrids)
Availability January to March; potted or garden
Price Cheap
Colour range White, cream, purple, lilac, yellow, bronze
Life span Short
The first crocuses are one of the first signs that winter is coming to an end. Bring potted bulbs indoors and plant in a basket or bowl.

CUPRESSUS (True cupress; *Cupressus glabra*)
Availability Year-round; cut
Price Cheap
Colour range Green, blue, gold
Life span Very long-lasting
Many different varieties of this foliage. Produces a cone, which varies in appearance. Good for Christmas arrangements and wreaths.

ELAEAGNUS (*Elaeagnus* spp.)
Availability Year-round; cut
Price Expensive, or free from garden
Colour range Yellow/green variegated foliage
Life span Very long-lasting
Deep gold foliage gives colour and interest in winter months when flowers are scarce. Grey underside to leaves can be displayed effectively in wired wedding bouquets.

EUCALYPTUS (*Eucalyptus gunnii*)
Availability Year-round; cut
Price Medium
Colour range Grey
Life span Very long-lasting
Native to Australia but easily grown in cooler climates. Silver-grey foliage; leaf size according to variety. Heavy, characteristic scent.

EUONYMUS (*Euonymus* sp.)
Availability Year-round; cut
Price Medium to expensive
Colour range Red, variegated, green
Life span Very long-lasting
Useful filler foliage. Dark green and variegated varieties are available from florists. Small shiny leaf on stiff branch.

EUPHORBIA (Spurge; *Euphorbia fulgens*)
Availability October to February; cut
Price Expensive
Colour range Cream, apricot, orange, red
Life span Long-lasting
Long slender stem, one-third covered with clusters of tiny flowers. Sap bleeds if flower or leaf is removed and can be a skin irritant. Useful in mixed arrangements or for extending the line of a display.

FREESIA (*Freesia* hybrids)
Availability Year-round; cut
Price Cheap to medium
Colour range White, cream, yellow, red, purple
Life span Long-lasting
Highly perfumed, and popular flower, sold in multicoloured bunches or in single colours. Long-stemmed varieties demand a higher price. Freesias look delicate on their own; also work well in wedding bouquets.

GLADIOLUS (Sword lily; *Gladiolus* hybrids)
Availability Year-round; cut
Price Cheap to medium
Colour range White, cream, orange, red, pink, purple, green, lilac, apricot
Life span Long-lasting
Large florets growing up stem. Unfortunate association with 1950's style. Looks supremely elegant in tall vases. Use individual florets in wedding work.

HEATHER (*Erica* sp.)
Availability Year-round; cut
Price Medium
Colour range White, pink, purple
Life span Long-lasting
Over 500 different varieties available for gardens; commercially only a few are supplied for the Christmas trade. Wonderful colours; adds texture to arrangements.

HOLLY (*Ilex aquifolium*)
Availability Year-round; cut
Price Medium
Colour range Green, variegated white or yellow
Life span Very long-lasting
Traditional Christmas foliage. Different coloured berries, ranging from yellow to red. Use in wreaths, for table centres and in mixed arrangements.

HYACINTH (*Hyacinthus orientalis* hybrids)
Availability December to April; cut or potted
Price Medium
Colour range White, apricot, cream, pink, blue
Life span Long-lasting
Beautifully perfumed bulb flower. Heavy flower head composed of small bell-like flowers. Individual florets are excellent wired in bouquets and headdresses.

IVY (*Hedera* spp.)
Availability Year-round; cut
Price Cheap or free
Colour range Green, variegated yellow, cream and grey-green
Life span Very long-lasting
Wide range of leaf shape, size and colour. Invaluable foliage throughout the year, particularly in winter. Trails are useful for wedding work or to break up the lines of an arrangement.

LACHENALIA (spp.)
Availability December to February; cut
Price Cheap
Colour range Yellow, orange (commercially grown variety)
Life span Long-lasting
Interesting blotchy stem, with tiny bells of yellow and orange, about 4-5 in (10-13cm) total length. Use in posies or arrangements; can look quite tropical.

LARCH (*Larix* sp.)
Availability Year-round
Price Medium
Colour range Bright green, gold, russet
Life span Long-lasting
Spiky bright green needles through summer; cones only in winter. Often covered with lichen and moss. Excellent for seasonal arrangements or to lend an Eastern quality to a display.

LAUREL (*Laurus nobilis*)
Availability Year-round; cut
Price Medium
Colour range Dark green
Life span Very long-lasting
Shiny oval leaf. Traditional foliage in Christmas arrangements.

LICHEN
Availability Year-round
Price Medium
Colour range Greys
Life span Everlasting
Lichen is a type of grey moss. Dries out but can be immersed in warm water to make it supple for use. Can be glycerined to keep it flexible, and also dyed, but the natural grey colour works well in winter arrangements.

LILY (*Lilium* spp.)
Availability Year-round; cut
Price Expensive
Colour range White, pink, apricot, yellow, red
Life span Very long-lasting
White lilies are traditional symbols of purity and popular for weddings and religious festivals. Red varieties are a good source of colour in the winter months.

MAGNOLIA (*Magnolia* spp.)
Availability Year-round; flowers in spring
Price Cheap
Colour range Dark green or burgundy leaves
Life span Everlasting
Large shiny leaf with suede-like underside. Preserve leaves with glycerine. Can dye colours to tone with Christmas displays.

MISTLETOE (*Viscum* sp., *Phoradendron* sp.)
Availability December; cut
Price Cheap
Colour range Light green leaf, white berry
Life span Long-lasting
The Christmas tradition of kissing under the mistletoe makes this a popular foliage for parties. Hang a large bunch over the entrance to a room, tied with a ribbon.

MOSS (various species)
Availability Year-round
Price Cheap
Colour range Greens
Life span Very long-lasting
Sphagnum moss has short wiry tendrils. Bind onto wreath frames to create background for foliage and flowers.

Bun moss has a velvety texture. Wide range of uses. Pack around base of flower arrangements or combine with pebbles in glass tanks. Carpet moss is composed of slightly longer grass-like fronds.

NARCISSUS (Narcissus hybrids)
Availability October to April; cut or potted
Price Cheap to expensive
Colour range White, cream, yellow, apricot, orange
Life span Short life
Over 8000 registered varieties, although much fewer are available commercially. Beautiful scented flower.

ORCHID (*Dendrobium* sp.)
Availability September to April; cut
Price Medium
Colour range White, yellow, purple, red
Life span Very long-lasting
Exotic appearance. Many tiny florets along the length of the stem. Wonderful lasting quality; useful in wedding work.

PINE (Blue pine; *Pinus* sp.)
Availability Year-round; cut or potted
Price Cheap to expensive
Colour range Green, gold, blue
Life span Very long-lasting
The mainstay of Christmas decorations, either as cut branches, wreaths or full-scale trees. Many different varieties. Needles are packed the length of branches. Different-shaped cones. Strong scent.

POINSETTIA (*Euphorbia polychroma*)
Availability November to February; potted
Price Medium to expensive
Colour range White, pink, peach, red
Life span Long-lasting
The Christmas flower. Mass pots to make a vivid display. Red remains the favourite shade. Cut from pots for arrangements; seal the ends of stems by holding in a flame for 2-5 seconds.

RANUNCULUS (*Ranunculus asiaticus*)
Availability December to June; cut
Price Cheap to expensive
Colour range White, yellow, pink, apricot, orange, red
Life span Very long-lasting
One of the buttercup family, but with many more petals than the wild species. Buy tightly-budded flowers just showing colour. They will open out fully. Heads often bend at the stem, but this is not a sign of age. One of my favourite flowers.

ROSE (*Rosa* hybrids)
Availability Year-round; cut
Price Cheap to expensive
Colour range White, cream, yellow, apricot, salmon pink, red
Life span Medium
Good quality roses are now available throughout the year thanks to the efforts of growers and improvements in transportation. Buy tightly budded. If stems are wrapped in plastic lining, check that foliage has not begun to sweat. If heads droop, trim stems at an angle, wrap tightly in newspaper and place in deep water for a couple of hours.

RUSCUS
Availability Year-round; cut
Price Medium to expensive
Colour range Green
Life span Very long-lasting
Three types are available. There is a variety with a short strong stem and small spiky leaf, a variety with a flatter larger leaf and a variety with a tall arched stem. Female varieties have orange berries.

SALIX (White willow; *Salix alba*)
Availability October to March; cut
Price Medium
Colour range Red, green with catkin
Life span Long-lasting
Bare branches can be used to create interesting colour and textural effects throughout winter. Many different varieties.

SNOWDROP (*Galanthus nivalis*)
Availability January to March; cut
Price Cheap
Colour range White
Life span Short
Delightful white bell-like flower, suspended on a fragile stem and surrounded by narrow leaves. Use simply to emphasize their fragility.

VIBURNUM (*Viburnum tinus*)
Availability October to April; cut
Price Medium
Colour range Pink-white flower, dark green leaf
Life span Very long-lasting
Pretty flower on sturdy branch. Good in large and small arrangements and wired for bridal work.

YEAR-ROUND FLOWERS
Although some of the following flowers and foliage are associated with a particular season, they are generally available year-round from florists and flower stalls, and make a useful supplement to the typical seasonal range.
*indicates description in text.

*ALSTROEMERIA	GYPSOPHILA
*BOX	IRIS
*CARNATION	*IVY
*CHRYSANTHEMUM	*LAUREL
*CUPRESSUS	*LILY
*EUCALYPTUS	*MOSS
*FREESIA	*ORCHID
*GLADIOLUS	*ROSE

A Style for Winter

There are two basic approaches to winter arrangements, both of which convey a seasonal atmosphere, but in a completely different way. The first builds on the traditional Christmas and New Year style of decorations, relying on rich combinations of evergreen, red berries and flowers, with additional elements such as fruits, nuts, fabric and branches. The aim of these designs is to create a sense of glowing colour and abundance which counteracts the barren quality of the winter landscape. One important dimension is scent — the tang of pine and citrus, the herbal smell of evergreen, the spicy odour of star-anise and cinnamon sticks give an unmistakable winter flavour.

At the other extreme, evocative winter displays can be created precisely by mirroring what is going on outside. Bare branches and twigs interspersed with a few precious flowers have a cool, spartan beauty which suits modern interiors particularly well.

Dried flowers can be used to achieve either of these two looks. Dried ingredients lend themselves to the compact designs — garlands, wreaths and posies — which are traditionally associated with winter celebrations. And the fragility of dried flowers can also be used to echo the muted quality of the winter landscape.

Above left: The warmth and intricacy of the paisley fabric has been accentuated by a collection of different coloured heathers, packed into a basket and surrounded by moss.

Right: Red is a colour very much associated with the Christmas season. Here red amaryllis, red ranunculus and lichen dyed red are set off by a mixture of winter foliage, including both green and variegated holly, ivy and bun moss.

COLOUR

Colour is undoubtedly an important way of conveying a seasonal mood. Certain shades and combinations of shades have very firm associations which link them to a particular time of year. In the case of winter, red and green is the cheering festive combination, supplemented by silver and gold. These sparkling, vital colours act as an antidote to grey days when light levels are low.

Bright colour combinations can be difficult to achieve easily in winter when flower varieties are limited. One solution is to spend money getting a good quantity of one variety of flower and introduce different colours with the container, some fabric, fruit or other accessories. Near, or clashing shades are more powerful than subtle coordination: red and pink, yellow and blue, pink and yellow, shocking pink and violet have an electric, jolting quality which makes them especially eye-catching in winter. This type of display is always more effective if it echoes at least one colour which is already present in the decoration of the room so that the combination has some kind of visual anchor.

No-colour is another winter strategy, either the washed-out pallor of dried flowers, the monochromatic effect of bare twigs, or the delicacy and purity of early spring blooms. Twigs can be sprayed white or silver for a frosty look. White heather, lilies, snowdrops and Christmas roses have a similar icy beauty.

POSITION

Extremes of temperature can be a problem for winter arrangements. Certain rooms or positions (close to a window pane, for example) may be just too cold, while positions near central heating outlets, blazing fires or warm ovens and hobs can shorten the life of fresh flowers considerably. Many flowers also object to draughts. Dried flowers, since they are not affected to such an extent by heat and humidity, can be very useful in winter.

Safety is another consideration. Do not place large or trailing displays directly in a main route where they may be easily upset. Ensure that substantial arrangements

Left: A group of rustic pottery containers creates the effect of an indoor garden. The large bowl is planted with crocus, its surface covered with bun moss and pebbles. There is also a vase of violets, accompanied by a mixture of foliage in the other jugs.

are placed securely on a level surface that will not tip over with the weight of the display.

Aesthetically, the key to positioning is eyeline. Mantelpieces suit arrangements that are meant to be viewed from standing height – as you come into a room, for example, or on occasions such as drinks parties where people will not be sitting down. Hallways and front doors are often good locations, since flowers, wreaths and greenery will provide a special welcome for visitors. For displays which combine flowers with fruit or vegetables, dining tables, sideboards and dressers are ideal. Coffee tables suit arrangements that need to be viewed from above, such as those where the flower heads have been cut low.

Mirrors provide a dramatic setting for garlands and wreaths. Any architectural detail – a bracket, archway, fanlight – which is itself worthy of attention, is also a good place for floral emphasis.

CONTAINERS

A good variety of different containers – in terms of size, shape and style – is essential for the flower arranger. But you do not have to spend a fortune amassing a selection of fine porcelain or crystal vases. Many highly effective and interesting containers can be improvised from humble everyday items, such as jugs, pots, baskets and bowls. Plastic florist's trays, saucers and plates make suitable reservoirs for oasis if the container is not intended to be on view; jam jars can be tucked inside baskets waterproofed with plastic. Inexpensive glass tanks or cylinders in different sizes suit many applications – except for displays consisting of those flowers which discolour water.

In the winter, when the flower range is limited and the emphasis may well be on different textures and shades of green, containers can be used to supply additional colour. A collection of similar containers in bright colours can add vitality to a simple display of foliage. Similarly, baskets can be piled in a heap and sprayed gold or bronze to give a dramatic effect to a display. In one sense, this represents the opposite approach to what

Right: A whole range of different materials and accessories can be used to supplement the limited variety of flowers in the winter months. Here poppies and anemones in cream, peach and salmon pink have been mixed with foliage, shells and tassels to create a striking table centre.

might be the case in the summer: the container is being used not so much as a foil for the flowers but more as a focal point in its own right.

Baskets strike a suitably rustic note for arrangements that set out to achieve an old-fashioned or country look. There is a wide range available, from fine painted wicker to the more rough-hewn, woven from coarse grasses, vines and even dried roots and herbs. Other garden-type containers, such as stone urns or leaded troughs can suggest a certain period quality, while shiny brass or copper containers make the most of candlelight and Christmas glitter. For a pure white winter look, choose simple glass cylinders filled with twigs sprayed silver and glass tanks planted with snowdrops, moss and pebbles.

TYPES OF ARRANGEMENT

By necessity, winter arrangements often concentrate more on texture and line than on flower form and colour. A display of branches, moss and bark is every bit as effective as a conventional vase of flowers, and more seasonal, too.

A surprising variety of effects can be created depending on the type of branches you choose. Contorted willow twigs, widely available commercially, have an exotic, almost Eastern quality. Mature apple branches are gnarled and often covered in tweedy lichen. Large twigs are slender and pliable, while dogwood is tinged red or yellow, giving a subtle colour accent.

Branches can be massed in simple containers or twigs knotted and twisted into different shapes. You can experiment with other ingredients to create a winter still-life: moss will add a velvety texture and vibrant green; logs, bark, pine cones and nuts all suggest the winter woodland. For a theatrical or festive look spray twigs gold, silver or white.

When creating a vase arrangement, it is often best to begin at the rim of the container, so that the stems of the outer flowers or branches provide support for the larger central flowers which will stand upright. Measure each flower or branch against the container to estimate how much to cut from the stem, laying the flower against the

Right: The wreath is a traditional form of decoration but, by varying the contents, it can be interpreted in a modern way to suit a more graphic setting. Here muslin has been combined with rather fierce-looking hawthorn branches, moss, lichen and cones tipped with white paint to create a stark, strong look.

container in the angle in which it will be used to arrive at the correct length.

Two conventions from traditional floristry are worth considering. One is to allow one and a half times the height of flowers to container. This gives stability to the display as well as a sense of proportion, and ensures that there is enough water so that the flowers get the nourishment they need. Another useful rule is to combine flowers or types of foliage in odd numbers – in threes, fives and sevens – which avoids the static look that even-numbered compositions can produce.

Many winter arrangements rely on a combination of flowers, foliage and fruit, a strategy which also works well in the autumn months. But to give a display a true winter look, avoid using the type of garden vegetables and fruit which are more suggestive of harvest time, such as russet apples, gourds and leafy green vegetables. Opt instead for winter berries, pine cones, shiny red apples, walnuts, pecans, satsumas and kumquats. Cinnamon sticks and star-anise can add an aromatic dimension.

Combined arrangements always demand a little more thought and skill. To be successful, there should be some affinity between the components, in terms of colour, texture, form or theme. And there are some mixtures it is better to avoid. Dried flowers do not go well with fresh ones, although they are excellent in displays of branches and twigs. Silk flowers do not work with dried ones. If you are trying to create a rustic effect with moss, nuts and wheatsheaves do not spoil the arrangement by placing it in a new, bleached basket. If you are making a structured modern display, using contorted willow twigs in a glass vase, large single blooms would be more in keeping with the style than, for example, spray chrysanthemums.

There are various techniques for attaching fruit, vegetables and nuts to a flower arrangement. Using such a variety of elements most of these displays are created in oasis or moss, rather than directly in water. This is because it is easier to position and anchor them around a fixed mould.

*Heavy fruits and vegetables can be anchored with lengths of sharpened garden cane. Insert the cane into the oasis at the angle in which you want the fruit to be displayed. For additional stability, insert heavy florist's wire through the fruit or vegetable and wind one end around the cane.

*Berries can be pinned in place with a hairpin or fine wire. Small berries need to be laid on a horizontal plane within the arrangement.

*Attach nuts with wire pushed into the shell or use a glue gun to stick wire to the outside. Wire can be cut at an angle to make a sharpened end.

Right: Another variation on the theme of the wreath: a ready-made base of roots and vines has been interwoven with twists of green broom, forming a rough bow, and decorated with dried red chilli peppers.

Midwinter Colour

Bright, cheerful colours are very important when days are dull. The shades in the vase have been echoed in the content of this display, apple green being the most prominent. This green is provided by a type of viburnum called gelder rose, a heavy blossom whose rounded shape helps to create a full arrangement.

FLOWERS AND FOLIAGE

Viburnum, Gelder rose (imported)
Pink alstroemeria
Yellow arum lilies
Solidago

MATERIALS

Vase

METHOD

1   Start by placing the shortest flowers on the rim of the vase. Build up the basic shape with solidago and gelder rose.
2   Next add the alstroemeria and finally the arum lilies, balancing these larger flowers within the flower framework.

CARE

Add a flower food to the water and top up often.

Cool Whites

A soft arrangement of white flowers, interspersed with plenty of greenery, softens the hard angles of this pure modern room without detracting from the clean, white decor. The glass vase echoes the transparency of the table.

FLOWERS AND FOLIAGE

Camellias
Longiflorum lilies
Viburnum, Gelder rose
Ivy
Fine green foliage

MATERIALS

Glass vase

METHOD

1. Start by placing short flowers and foliage against the rim of the vase.
2. Gradually build up the height, using more delicate fronds of foliage towards the edge.
3. Use a longer strand of foliage to one side to create an extended line and repeat at the top of the display.

CARE

Change the water regularly. A flower food will prolong the life of the display but will discolour the water.

Snowdrops

Snowdrops are one of the few flowers to appear in winter. They are normally fairly inexpensive to buy in quantity, but can be difficult to use because their stems are too frail for inserting into oasis. Here small vases massed within a basket have been surrounded with moss to suggest the effect of flowers growing naturally.

FLOWERS AND FOLIAGE

Snowdrops
Ivy leaves
Moss

MATERIALS

Basket
Small glass vases or jam jars
Plastic lining
Pebbles

METHOD

1   Gather the stems of the snowdrops together. Place ivy leaves at the base of each bunch, towards the edge. Put into small water-filled jars.
2   Place the jars in a basket that has been lined with plastic.
3   Pack moss around the jars and decorate the surface with a scattering of pebbles.

CARE

Change the water in the jars regularly.

Pink Basket

Dried flowers need not make faded displays. This basket arrangement consists of closely massed and segregated varieties which intensifies the pretty pink shades of the dried summer flowers. Massing is also important for smaller arrangements.

FLOWERS AND FOLIAGE

Dried larkspur
Dried roses
1 dried peony
Rose foliage

MATERIALS

Basket
Dried flower oasis
Waterproof tape

METHOD

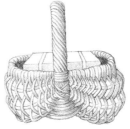

1   Grasp the flowers into small individual bunches according to varieties. Leave ¾-1 in (2-2.5 cm) bare stems.
2   Start in the centre at the highest point and work down. Push bunches of flowers and clusters of foliage into oasis.
3   Place the open peony in a prominent position.

CARE

No care is required.

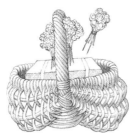

Vivid Still Life

When flowers are expensive and scarce, it is best to combine them with other elements, such as vegetables and fruit, to create tableaux reminiscent of traditional still lifes. Blues can look cold, but when mixed with greens and purples they take on a richer and warmer appearance.

FLOWERS AND FOLIAGE

Tulips
Violets
Heather
Laurel leaves
Winter cabbage
Apples
Grapes

MATERIALS

Dinner plate
Oasis
Small canes
Water vials

METHOD

1   Place a block of soaked oasis on a dinner plate. Insert a cane into the cabbage and then into the oasis.
2   Gradually build upwards, using grapes and apples towards the top. Hold the fruit in position with canes.
3   Position water vials containing bunches of violets, tulips and heather.
4   Open out the petals of a group of tulips to give the flowers a different look.

CARE

Change the water in the vials and water the oasis daily.

Christmas Garland

This garland has been composed primarily of dried summer flowers but the colours have been selected to suggest Christmas: reds, silvery greys and blues. Garlands can be used to decorate mirrors, mantelpieces or as table centres.

FLOWERS AND FOLIAGE

Purple lavender
Red miniature spray roses
Grey lichen
Pink dried flowers
Moss

MATERIALS

Florist's wire

METHOD

1   Ensure that the moss is dry. Mould the moss into a sausage shape and bind tightly with wire. Each loop of wire should be about ½ in (1.5 cm) apart. The final width will depend on the size of garland you require; in this case, the moss is about 2 in (5 cm) wide.
2   Cut dried flowers to about 2½ in (6.5 cm) in length and make small bunches by wiring with lengths of florist's wire. (Use the double-leg mount method – see p.109). The heads of the flowers should all face in the same direction as you attach them to the moss.
3   Insert the bunches into the moss, alternating varieties. Pin clumps of lichen in between the hairpins of wire.

CARE

No after-care is required.

Colour Accent

Containers can supply a good deal of the colour interest during the winter months when flower varieties are more limited. The brilliant blue of this vase makes a sharp contrast to the yellow and orange flowers.

FLOWERS AND FOLIAGE

Alstroemeria
Orange lilies
Orange euphorbia
Yellow arums
Solidago
Catkins
Foliage from castor oil plant

MATERIALS

Vase

METHOD

1   Start by placing two large leaves on the rim of the vase.
2   Gradually add flowers, building upwards in height.
3   Add catkins. Finally place last two stems of alstroemeria so that they balance between the catkin branches.

CARE

Check the water and change as required.

Winter Tree

A "tree" of moss and twigs can make a striking alternative to a traditional Christmas tree, or as an arrangement throughout the winter. Colours and materials echo the mood of the winter landscape. To give the tree a natural look, it is important to ensure that the stem is thick enough to appear in proportion to the pot and sphere of moss.

FLOWERS AND FOLIAGE

Moss
Birch twigs
Log

MATERIALS

Terracotta pot
Quick-drying cement
Florist's wire

METHOD

1 Cement the log into the pot.
2 When the cement is dry, attach one end of a reel of wire to the top of the log and begin to bind on the moss. This is a fairly lengthy process. Work until you have achieved a spherical shape.
3 Take several twigs and twist so that they entwine. Use the double-leg mount method (see p. 109) to secure them at each end and insert into the moss. Decorate top of pot with moss.

CARE

No extra care is required.

Ceramic Collection

A collection of sculptural ceramics needed to be complemented, rather than overwhelmed, by the flower display. The sharp yellow brings out the gold detail on the ceramics and combines well with the blue-grey finish; ivy berries exaggerate the pitted surface of the pots. The whole display is fairly low so as not to obscure the form of the ceramics.

FLOWERS AND FOLIAGE

Yellow arum lilies
Solidago
Grey brullia (protea family)
Leaves from castor oil plant
Flowering ivy (*Hedera helix arborescens*)

MATERIALS

Ceramic pots

METHOD

1 Group varieties together. Cut stems so that all heads are level and sit groups low, resting on the rims of the pots. Place each variety in a different container.
2 Surround the brullia with a large leaf.
3 Insert long arums into the container at the rear, balancing among the solidago.

CARE

Check the water daily and change as necessary.

Study in Texture

The beauty of many dried materials lies in their texture. Here a grouping of various types of cones, walnuts, brazils and driftwood has been used to emphasize the quality of a fine carved mirror frame. The display can be polished with varnish to give added lustre.

FLOWERS AND FOLIAGE

Cones
Driftwood
Nuts
Ivy

MATERIALS

Heavy florist's wire
Glue gun

METHOD

1   Twist wire around cones, leaving long ends. Use a glue gun to attach wires to nuts.
2   When all the components have been wired, twist the wires together, working in one direction.
3   Entwine fresh green ivy through the short garland.

CARE

No further care is required. The ivy will deteriorate but can be replaced easily.

Country Garland

A dried flower garland is draped across a country kitchen dresser, the colours of the flowers harmonizing with the pretty floral patterned china. Dried flower displays really come into their own during the winter, providing a welcome reminder of warm weather and summer abundance.

FLOWERS AND FOLIAGE

Spray roses
Hydrangea
Lavender

MATERIALS

Florist's wire
String

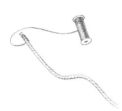

METHOD

1 Cut a piece of string to the required length of the garland and attach one end to a reel of wire.
2 Cut flowers to about 6 in (15 cm) in length. Group in small bunches.
3 Attach flowers, binding to the string and overlapping as you go with new bunches of flowers, all pointing in the same direction.
4 Continue to the end of the string.

CARE

No care is required. If the garland becomes dusty, you can clean it by gently blowing off the dust with a hair dryer.

Winter Weddings

Seasonal flowers provide a ready-made theme which gives a special unity and atmosphere to a wedding day. The dresses of the bride and her attendants, the decorations in the church and at the reception, and even the type of refreshments served should in some way acknowledge the time of year.

Winter weddings, in particular, need a strong, seasonal link. Rich, bright flower colours are better than pale pastels on dark cold days, complementing the complexion and injecting a sense of vitality into gloomy interiors. Flowers are a natural means of projecting a feeling of warmth.

For weddings which take place towards the end of the year there is an inevitable association with Christmas, which can be perpetuated by adopting a traditional style of decoration, using evergreen and berries. After the New Year, it is more effective to create a white or silvery winter look or to suggest an early spring with dainty bulb flowers. Whichever approach you adopt, keeping within the limits of the season will be practical as well as visually effective: recreating summer abundance in the depths of winter is an expensive proposition.

Above left: Dried flower circlets and posies suit the winter mood of nostalgia. Dried versions of favourite summer flowers can give a wedding bouquet a special meaning. This circlet and posy consists of dried roses, larkspur, nigella seedheads and rose leaves.

Right: A pure white winter look, with a pungent herbal scent. This wired posy includes a mixture of different pines – which accounts for its wonderful smell – along with holly, ivy, viburnum, white dill, wax flowers and white roses.

CHOOSING WEDDING FLOWERS

Although there are few problems with overheating or wilting in the winter, certain flowers will simply not last well in bouquets or headdresses if they are wired. A bouquet can take an hour and a half to make and must often be delivered to the bride at least two hours before the wedding so that there is enough time for the hairdresser and photographer to do their work. This means that by the time the wedding party is ready for the ceremony, the flowers will already have been out of water for nearly four hours. Appropriate flowers are best chosen in consultation with a florist, who will be able to advise on suitability.

I am often asked how to preserve a bouquet as a keepsake. Many bouquets can be successfully dried by immersing them in silica gel (crystals) (page 108). An alternative is to opt for a dried flower bouquet. All of the dried flowers listed on page 106 are suitable for wedding work.

Left: This simple tied posy in warm vibrant colours would suit a registry office wedding. Anemones are combined with eucalyptus and skimmia.

SUITABLE WINTER FLOWERS AND FOLIAGE

Alstroemeria   Delicate, expensive and exotic-looking, but relatively cheap. Lasts well, even when wired.

Amaryllis   Large trumpet flowers have a dramatic look.

Anemone   Intense, vivid shades. Handle with care if using in wired bouquets.

Carnation   Cheap, long-lasting and perfumed. 'Shatter' the large heads to wire into bouquets and give a more delicate look.

Chrysanthemum   Solid, long-lasting flower. Single varieties are better. Use rich bronzes and dark reds.

Elaeagnus   Good wedding foliage. Grey underside equally effective.

Eucalyptus   Silver-grey foliage looks wintry.

Euphorbia   Delicate flowers similar to orange blossom. Use as trails or wired in bouquets.

Freesia   All-round popular wedding flower. Excellent colour range, very scented.

Gladiolus   Use individual florets rather than whole stems.

Heather   Useful source of colour; gives a sense of fluidity to bouquets. White heather is traditionally lucky.

Helleborus   Cut the thick stem low and use the flower open in wired bouquets.

Holly   Shiny, hardy leaf. Use the 'female' holly which is not prickly.

Hyacinth   Useful source of blue. Good scent. Use individual bells rather than whole stem.

Ivy   Invaluable foliage for trails and in bouquets.

Lily   Long-lasting and dramatic. Available in seasonal reds and white.

Mistletoe   White berries look charming in headdresses and circlets. Romantic association.

Orchid   Vibrant colours and exotic appearance.

Pine   Range of blue-greys and silver as well as green. Herbal scent.

Ranunculus   Drooping head gives a sense of movement. Old-fashioned appearance.

Rose   Use warm red shades or pure white.

Snowdrop   Dainty flower. Rather frail; use tied in bunches with stems left on.

THE BRIDE'S FLOWERS

The bride is the focus of attention throughout the wedding. Her flowers should be considered first and used as the basis for the colour and style of the other displays. In practice, this means selecting the flowers and planning the design of the bouquet and headdress once the bride's dress has been chosen.

On a winter's day, it is important to look and feel warm. Winter wedding dresses should not be too flimsy, low cut or diaphanous, otherwise you run the risk of being uncomfortable and looking inappropriate. Heavier fabric such as velvet, brocade, and textured silk is better than fine tulle, lace or chiffon. Necklines can be higher, sleeves longer and styles layered to incorporate a shawl, wrap or jacket. Hoods, cowls and sari-type veils can provide extra warmth.

The bride's flowers should not only reinforce the sense of warmth but also make some kind of seasonal statement. For a rich, natural bouquet, you could assemble a combination of pine cones, roses, holly berries and leaves. Mistletoe makes a charming and witty addition to a headdress. Hellebores and miniature red roses create a striking 'snow queen' combination.

Dried flowers tend to have a nostalgic appeal and work well in traditional designs. These are not fluid or robust enough for trailing displays but lend themselves to compact shapes such as circlets, posies, garlands and pomanders.

FLOWERS FOR THE ATTENDANTS

To maintain a sense of unity, flowers for the bride's attendants and the wedding party should reflect those selected for the bride, either by coordinating colour, design of the bouquet or type of flower. Wide differences of style can lead to visual chaos.

Adult bridesmaids can carry a smaller and less elaborate version of the bridal bouquet, perhaps with subtle colour variations. Male family members might like to choose a flower from the bride's bouquet for their buttonholes; women can wear corsages incorporating some of the bridal flowers.

Right: Rich colours add warmth to winter weddings. The clashing pinks and reds of this wired bouquet are set off by a variety of winter foliage. Contents include heather, roses, elaeagnus, cupressus, pine, ivy and cones.

Little bridesmaids and pages are always delightful. Their flowers need not be coordinated with the bride's to such a degree, although it is always more effective to stick to the same general type and overall colour scheme. Children, however, should not be given overly sophisticated bouquets. They need flowers which are fun to carry, easy to manage and which suit them rather than reinforce the importance of the occasion. For a traditional wedding, child attendants can carry little baskets filled with dried flowers; pomanders, garlands and posies also work well on a smaller scale. A Victorian look can be created by trimming muffs with ivy, greenery and tiny flowers; a hat decorated with sprigs of foliage might be warmer and more seasonal than a headdress.

FLOWERS FOR THE CEREMONY AND RECEPTION

In general, during the winter months, the range of affordable flowers is rather limited, particularly considering the amount you may need to decorate a large space such as a church or synagogue, or wherever the reception is held. As in the autumn, the solution is to rely on foliage to create a sense of textural depth and to use fruit, nuts and candles to supply additional colour and atmosphere. It is also important to be more inventive with shape.

Dark green holly, variegated ivy, blue pine and gold elaeagnus make a vivid foliage combination which can be used to dress pew ends, make entrance wreaths or garlands that wind down a staircase. Foliage displays can be trimmed with holly berries and sprayed cones for extra colour. For a winter, as distinct from a Christmas wedding, silvery branches, the starlike flowers of winter jasmine and early spring flowers have a shimmering beauty, especially when picked out by candlelight.

Dried flowers are invaluable for winter wedding displays. If you plan ahead, favourite flowers from the summer garden can be dried and set aside for a wedding later in the year – a solution which is both economical and meaningful. Pot pourri or dried rose petals can be sprinkled up the aisle for a scented, colourful pathway.

Left: A trio of little Christmas bridesmaids carry simple tied bunches of red anemones surrounded by glossy ivy leaves. The circlets also feature anemones, with blue pine, ivy and cupressus; the garland is a mixture of seasonal foliage.

Containers often need to be more obvious and interesting to make up for the lack of flower variety. Old chimney pots look rustic and forthright; shiny brass or copper troughs make the most of light.

Potted plants are another way of extending the possibilities. Cinerarias, in deep velvety colours, are particularly effective; poinsettias strike an appropriately festive note. At church and at home, a Christmas tree makes a natural focal point for a winter wedding.

In church, always ask permission before attaching floral decorations, garlands or wreaths to fixtures. If your budget is limited, concentrate your best efforts on one or two large displays, positioned where they will have most impact and visibility – at the alter and at the entrance. Pew end decorations should not obstruct the view.

At the reception, as at any party, displays should be large enough to be seen from a distance, with flowers grouped in clusters of three or more to increase their impact. Avoid floor-level arrangements, which will only get in the way and remember to decorate the key positions – the entrance, the main tables and around the cake – all places where people will naturally congregate and photographs are likely to be taken.

Below left: When flowers are expensive and variety is limited, you may have to rely on contrasts of texture and on the different shapes and shades of foliage to create interest. This hanging decoration for a pew end or church fitting includes a few white anemones, some preserved fungi and catkins, as well as foliage.

Right: Flower decorations for wedding receptions should be fairly large and obvious. One big display is better than a few small ones, dotted about the room. This dramatic pedestal arrangement combines poppies, anemones and orange euphorbia with shells and tassels for a richly decorative look.

Snowdrop Posy

A simple tied posy of snowdrops looks fresh and impromptu and makes a charming winter bridal bouquet. Other flowers could be used to create a similar effect.

FLOWERS AND FOLIAGE

Snowdrops
Ivy leaves

MATERIALS

Twine
Ribbon

METHOD

1 Group a handful of snowdrops together. Tie with twine.
2 Gradually add small bunches of flowers, working in a circular way around the central bunch until you make a round dome shape.
3 Edge with large green ivy leaves and cover the string with ribbon.
4 Cut stems level.

CARE

The posy can be refreshed at intervals during the day by placing it in a vase of water.

Pew End Decoration

A pew end for a winter wedding uses seasonal components which are affordable as well as effective. Terracotta pots add a touch of country charm while the garland serves to guide guests to their seats. Always take care when attaching decorations to church fittings and make sure you ask permission first.

FLOWERS AND FOLIAGE

Pine
Ivy
Holly
Nuts or fruit

MATERIALS

String
Reel of florist's wire
Plastic tray
Oasis
Terracotta pots
Canes
Waterproof tape
Glue gun

METHOD

1 To make the garland, first cut a length of string to the required length. Attach wire to the end of the string and make a loop large enough to encircle the pew end. Soak oasis in water.
2 Gradually add pieces of foliage cut to about 6 in (15 cm) long, binding with wire as you go. Work in one direction. At the other end of the string, make another loop of wire to encircle the second pew end.
3 Use waterproof tape to attach soaked oasis to the plastic tray and attach tray to pew end.
4 Starting from the bottom, insert trails upwards into the foam, and gradually build up and out. Insert three pots with canes, resting them on top of each other. Fill pots with nuts or fruit.
5 Fill in with foliage. Decorate garland with nuts bound on with wire attached with glue gun.

CARE

Water the oasis carefully.

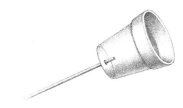

Christmas Pedestal

You can create an impressive display, easily visible from the back of the church, using only a few flowers. Attractive, reusable props, such as terracotta pots and a pedestal, form the basis for an arrangement which relies on seasonal plants and foliage.

FLOWERS AND FOLIAGE

Single red chrysanthemums
Anemones
Cineraria plants
Moss
Foliage

MATERIALS

Pedestal
Terracotta pots
Oasis
Canes
Wire
Waterproof tape
Waterproof container

METHOD

1   Build up a depth of oasis in the pedestal so that it comes about 12 in (31 cm) over the rim. Tape into position.
2   Starting from the tallest point, insert the tall stems of foliage, working one-third from the back of the pot. Build out on the sides at angles. At the lower level, add chrysanthemums.
3   Insert canes through pots and insert in oasis. Add cineraria plants, packing around with moss. Do the same with the anemones, using a container that will hold water. Insert trails to cover the base of the container.
4   Bind bare branches with wire. Insert cane and insert into oasis diagonally. Fill gaps with moss and foliage.

CARE

Water daily.

68

Double Rose Buttonhole

Making a change from the usual carnation, this classic man's buttonhole consists of two white roses. Additional interest has been supplied by various types of foliage.

FLOWERS AND FOLIAGE

Two white roses
Ivy leaves
Twigs

MATERIALS

Fine silver wire
Heavier steel wire
Self-sealing florist's tape.

METHOD

1   Remove most of the stem from the two roses, leaving about ½ in (1.5 cm). Insert heavy wire through the seedhead. Bend ½ in (1.5 cm) down. This replaces removed stem. Cover with tape.
2   Remove the stems from the ivy leaves, leaving about ½ in (1.5 cm). Insert fine silver wire into the foliage, about one-third from the tip of the leaf, across the centre vein. Make a small stitch. Pull the wires down and twist around the remaining stem. Cover with tape.
3   Wind a small bunch of twigs with wire and place behind the roses, taping together. Add one leaf at the rear of the roses, one in front of the second rose. Tape and cut wires to required length.
5   Completely cover the wire "stems" with tape so that no ends protrude which could catch on clothing.

CARE

The buttonhole will last well all day.

Special Occasions

Winter is dominated by the Christmas and New Year festivities – a time of year when few people feel self-conscious about decorating their homes with flowers and foliage. There is something innately nostalgic about these celebrations – traditions and continuity are important and the past is a rich source of inspiration.

Since the holidays are so long, it really is worth the extra effort and expense to create a memorable display, whether you are planning a special party or expecting the family to arrive. Restraint is inappropriate: the best decorations are uninhibited and exuberant.

Left: Candles are particularly evocative of the Christmas season. This grouping of church candles has been fixed to a traditional wreath base of blue pine, holly and cones to make a glowing table centre.

Right: The fireplace is often the focal point of winter parties. This mantelpiece display is a softened version of the traditional triangular-shaped arrangement, with varieties grouped and massed to emphasize textural contrast. Pine, ivy, laurel and preserved magnolia leaves are combined with dried poppy heads, red lichen, carnations and anemones.

CHRISTMAS TRADITIONS

Many of our Christmas traditions to do with flowers and greenery are rooted deep in the unchristian past. The custom of bringing evergreen branches indoors is an ancient one, originating in the pagan ceremonies surrounding the winter solstice. Evergreen was a symbol of continuing life when other trees were bare and leaves were brown. Holly, ivy and mistletoe were particularly venerated because they continued to produce berries even in the depths of winter. The Romans also gave green branches and holly as presents at this time of year for their midwinter festival.

Mistletoe has always been very powerful in folklore, as a protection against evil, a poison remedy and a fertility symbol — which is perhaps where today's association with kissing comes from. Holly and yew were thought to protect against witches and the evil eye.

The tradition of hanging wreaths on the front door came from Scandinavia. Wreaths were tokens of renewal, peace and friendship. Other Christmas decorations which originated in Scandinavian countries are wreaths, braids, figures and stars woven from straw — all ancient fertility symbols.

Rosemary — "for remembrance" — was once very popular as a Christmas decoration but fell out of favour in the nineteenth century, about the time when the Christmas tree was widely adopted in Britain. And the custom of keeping flowering plants at Christmas time — such as pots of hyacinths and poinsettias — arose from the legend that trees burst into flower on the first Christmas Eve.

CHRISTMAS TREE DECORATIONS

Few households are without a tree at Christmas — the focal point of family traditions year to year. But their popularity was not always so widespread. Christmas trees had long been a part of the German Christmas celebrations when Prince Albert, consort of Queen Victoria, introduced them to the English court in the 1840s. Today, they are one of the most recognizable symbols of Christmas all over the world.

Left: An opulent Christmas garland or swag makes a long-lasting decoration for the holiday period. Holly, moss, pine and cones are wired onto a moss base, with bright red apples and tangerines interspersed with red velvet. The decoration should last about three weeks, although the fruit may need to be changed earlier.

Fir trees sold at Christmas time come in a wide price range, which reflects their longevity, density of needles and, often, their colour. The variety which has tightly-packed needles and a bluish tinge has been very popular in recent years, but does tend to be more expensive since the needles stay on longer. Pot-grown trees can usually be replanted, but not all trees which are sold in pots have been pot-grown. Many have been uprooted from a plantation, and their roots trimmed before being planted in a pot. These rarely can be replanted successfully. All cut trees will lose their needles, a process which is accelerated by warm, centrally-heated rooms.

Christmas trees generally look more dramatic and effective if decorations follow some type of theme. Colour is an obvious choice. White, red, gold and silver are popular colour themes. Other ideas include:
*an aromatic tree, decorated with star-anise, cinnamon sticks, muslin bags filled with cloves, orange peel curls and sheaves of lavender.
*a toy tree, hung with tiny horns, rocking horses, tin drums and striped candy canes.
*an edible tree, with pretzels, iced biscuits, candy canes, wrapped sweets, fruit, nuts and strings of popcorn.
*a folk art tree, featuring handmade painted wooden ornaments from Mexico, India or Russia in brilliant clashing colours.

PARTY DECORATIONS AND TABLE SETTINGS

For any special occasion, flower decorations need to be somewhat exaggerated – bolder, more dramatic and larger than usual – to make an impact. If your budget is tight, concentrate on one big display rather than a few small arrangements which might be overlooked. Remember to position displays well out of the way, but in a place where they can be seen and appreciated easily.

Winter parties which take place towards the end of the year inevitably acquire a Christmas theme. Garlands, door wreaths and Christmas trees are all appropriately seasonal and festive. Decorations after the New Year can have a wintry theme or even suggest an early spring.

Right: A preserved garland can be used year after year, and makes a striking decoration for a mirror, fireplace or tabletop. Here preserved magnolia leaves, dyed aubergine, red amaranthus and cones have been bound onto a piece of rope which is simply draped in place.

Table settings enhance any dinner party, provided they are low enough not to obstruct views and inhibit conversation. At Christmas time, there is often so much food on the table that there is barely any room for a flower arrangement. If this is the case, you can decorate plates and platters instead. A roast goose or turkey can be encircled with a wreath of foliage combined with fresh cranberries, apricots, chestnuts and prunes – all the better if you can use ingredients from the stuffing. The Christmas pudding plate can be trimmed with holly.

A table centre comprised largely of foliage can incorporate little baskets or pots to hold sweets, nuts and fruit. Napkins can be tied with ivy trails, sprayed gold; green and white variegated ivy looks stunning pinned to a snowy white tablecloth. For a really theatrical look, build a table setting with cones, apples, fruit and candles all sprayed silver or gold.

GIFTS

Dried flowers make the perfect winter gift, as they are long-lasting and need absolutely no care. Fresh flowers are welcome at any time of the year, but in winter you may have to accept a more limited choice. Whether you choose a fresh or dried selection, it is always worth spending the time to make your present personal and meaningful. Think about the person who will receive the flowers – their favourite colours, personality and style. With a little effort and perhaps some advice from a florist, flowers can become a really special gift.

Spiralled or tied bunches are particularly welcome as thank-you presents or gifts to a host or hostess. As they are ready to go straight into water, there is no need to spare valuable time arranging them. Tied bunches are also a good choice for hospital visits. But avoid perfumed flowers; in a confined space, heavy scent can be overwhelming.

Flowers work well with other presents. Tie Christmas parcels with sprays of dried lavender and red roses, or make a decoration with cones and ivy leaves sprayed silver or gold. You can also fill a basket with little gifts and wrap the handle with trails of ivy and tiny flowers.

Right: Topiary makes a good alternative to a traditional Christmas tree and is much better than artificial designs. The base of the "tree" is a wooden trunk, covered with sphagnum moss. Bun moss is pinned on top to create the tree shape. The tree is decorated with cinnamon sticks, nuts, dried roses and kumquats wired in place. Only the fresh kumquats will need to be replaced.

Heraldic Device

A collection of heraldic shields on a simple white background has been accentuated by bunches of burgundy grapes and a garland of dark laurel leaves. A wreath to match decorates the fireplace recess.

FLOWERS AND FOLIAGE

Laurel
Pine
Conifer branches
Grapes

MATERIALS

String
Reel of wire
Wreath frame
Cut lengths of florist's wire

METHOD

1   To make the garland: cut foliage into 6-8 in (15-20 cm) pieces. Attach one end of the reel of wire to the end of a piece of string, cut to the required length.
2   Bind on foliage, overlapping tops over stems. Work from one end of the string to the centre, then start at the other end until you meet at the middle.
3   To make the wreath: attach wire from the reel onto wreath frame. Lay 4 in (10 cm) pieces of foliage onto the frame and bind on, overlapping as you go and working all in one direction.
4   To attach the grapes: hook lengths of wire through each bunch and twist to create a hook. Attach to garland and wreath once they have been hung in position.

CARE

Spray foliage with a water spray from time to time.

Candlelit Table

The natural elements of glass and wood in the room suggest a display where the contents are similarly pure and simple: white muslin, driftwood, ivy and pine. The candles are slow-burning church candles, available from ecclesiastical suppliers.

FLOWERS AND FOLIAGE

Cones
Driftwood
Dried poppy seedheads
Blue pine
Ivy
Lichen-covered hawthorn twigs
Lichen
Moss

MATERIALS

Metal bowl
Oasis
Church candles
Tape
Florist's wire
Plastic lining
Muslin

METHOD

1 Tape two hairpins of wire to the base of the candles, making four prongs per candle. Place two soaked blocks of oasis in the bowl, which has been lined with plastic. Insert candles at different heights.
2 Place trails of pine and ivy towards the sides, resting them against the rim of the bowl. Build up groups of dried poppy heads towards the base of the candles.
3 Secure driftwood with hairpins of wire. Attach wire to cones and mass a group to one side. Pin moss and lichen to cover gaps.
4 Insert hawthorn twigs behind candles. Twist a length of muslin and pin between groupings.

CARE

Water oasis slightly each day to supply moisture for the pine and ivy.

Classic Door Wreath

Wreaths are always welcoming, but particularly at Christmas time. Designed to be in keeping with the strong classical lines of the entrance and the gun-metal colour of the door, this wreath of magnolia leaves is not overly fussy or decorated. A bow of hammered metal gives a look of sober dignity.

FLOWERS AND FOLIAGE

Preserved magnolia leaves
Moss

MATERIALS

Wire
Wreath frame
Reel of wire
Hairpins of florist's wire
Metal or fabric bow

METHOD

1   Attach wire to the wreath frame and bind moss on with loops set about ½in (1.5cm) apart.
2   Pin on the leaves. Work the outside edge first, then the inside edge, then the centre.
3   Insert bow into moss with wire.

CARE

No further care is necessary.

Christmas Swag

This full opulent-looking swag has a solid base of moss so that all the elements are wired in place. This type of decoration could be stored and reused from year to year.

FLOWERS AND FOLIAGE

Preserved magnolia leaves
Dyed green lichen
Amaranthus
Large natural cones
Small gold painted cones
Sphagnum moss (dry)

MATERIALS

Canes
Reel of wire
Florist's wire
Fabric
Ribbon
Rope
Small ornaments

METHOD

1   Make the frame to the required size by binding lengths of cane at right angles with rope. Attach one end of the reel of wire to the frame and bind on the moss, overlapping as you go. Space loops of wire about ½in (1.5cm) apart.
2   Wire cones, twisting the wire through the centres. Hairpin leaves around the edges of the swag. Work from each end until you meet in the centre.
3   Add bunches of amaranthus, using the double-leg mount method (see p. 109). Cluster cones from top to bottom down the centre of the moss. Fill in with twists of fabric, ribbon and clumps of grey lichen.

CARE

No extra care is required.

Winter Greenery

This grand display of winter greenery demands a large room to be fully appreciated. By using just foliage and candles an impressive arrangement can be created without spending too much money. This display would be ideal for a special dinner or for the duration of the holidays.

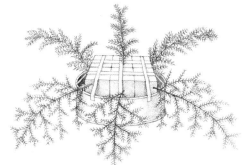

FLOWERS AND FOLIAGE

Laurel
Pine
Green and variegated ivy
Lichen-covered branches
Moss
Holly
Driftwood
Cones tipped with white paint

MATERIALS

Large bowl
Six blocks of oasis
Waterproof tape
Florist's wire
Candles

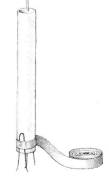

METHOD

1 Fill a bowl with oasis so that the oasis protrudes about 8 in (20 cm) over the rim. Tape in place.
2 Attach wire to candles with tape. Wire driftwood into position.
3 Insert the first pieces of foliage one-third from the back of the oasis, then fill in at both sides, at the front and between the two side pieces. Lean foliage back to keep the balance. Gradually fill into the centre with shorter pieces of foliage.
4 Insert candles in centre, packing with moss. Insert wood and cones in the centre. Sit other candles firmly on the surface.

CARE

Water oasis carefully every day. *Never leave lighted candles unattended because of the risk of fire.*

Fruit Bowl

Decorating dishes and platters with flowers and foliage is a good idea for the Christmas table, which can get too crowded for a full-scale flower arrangement. This holiday fruit bowl is trimmed with a garland and edged with laurel leaves.

FLOWERS AND FOLIAGE

Laurel
Pine
Cupressus
Cones
Holly
Moss
Fruit and nuts

MATERIALS

Large plate
Wire
String
Reel of wire
Tape

METHOD

1 Cut laurel leaves from the branches. Lay them on the edge of the plate and tape in place.
2 Cut a piece of string to encircle the plate. Bind moss onto string with the reel of wire. Use the double-leg mount (see p. 109) to bind 3 in (8 cm) pieces of foliage, fruit and cones. Insert these into the moss garland. Overlap the foliage, working in one direction.
3 Lay the garland onto the plate, covering the ends of the laurel leaves. Fill in the centre with fruit and nuts.

CARE

The decoration will last about 10 days without care.

Topiary Trees

These long-lasting small topiary trees can be used as a table centre or just as general decoration. Group with other festive things for a Christmas display. The trees can be made in different shapes.

FLOWERS AND FOLIAGE

Sphagnum moss
Bun moss
Cut lengths of wooden branches

MATERIALS

Pots
Quick-setting cement
Florist's wire
Glue
Reel of wire
Plastic lining

METHOD

1   Line the pots with plastic. Mix cement, tip into pots and place wooden 'logs' in the centres.
2   When the cement is dry, attach one end of the reel of wire to the log and bind on sphagnum moss to create a round ball.
3   Cut florist's wire and bend into hairpins 2 in (5 cm) long. Pin pieces of bun moss onto the round ball to make a smooth surface.
4   Glue moss on top of pots to cover the cement.

CARE

These trees last indefinitely and require no care.

Christmas Eve

Decorating a bed with winter foliage makes a magical scene for the night before Christmas. A large red bow provides the finishing touch.

FLOWERS AND FOLIAGE

Pine
Holly
Cupressus

MATERIALS

Reel of florist's wire
Large bow

METHOD

1   Attach wire to post or rail of bed or to a basic frame made of wood.
2   Start at the bottom, binding on long lengths of foliage. Work upwards, overlapping as you go.
3   Attach bow and add presents.

CARE

No care is needed.

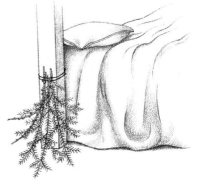

Pot Pourri Basket

Pot pourri is widely available and comes in a variety of scents, including the seasonal mixture of cinnamon, pine and cloves. To create an interesting container for pot pourri, decorate a basket with a garland of foliage and ribbon.

FLOWERS AND FOLIAGE	MATERIALS
Pot pourri	Reel of wire
Cones	Florist's wire
Pine	Basket
Bun moss	Ribbon
Sphagnum moss	Piece of sacking or hessian

METHOD

1. Attach reel of wire to the rim of the basket. Lay clumps of sphagnum moss on the rim of the basket and stitch in place with wire.
2. Wire cones into moss. Use double-leg mount (see p. 109) to attach 2 in (5 cm) pieces of foliage. Overlap foliage, working in one direction.
3. Pin on bun moss. Insert groupings of cones.
4. When the rim of the basket is fully covered, twist a ribbon through, tucking and pinning with hairpins of florist's wire.
5. Line the basket with sacking and fill with pot pourri.

CARE

No care required.

Basic Techniques

All cut flowers will last longer if they are properly trimmed and conditioned before arrangement; some species have special needs in this respect. In addition, there are various simple techniques, widely used by florists, which can extend the creative scope. One word of caution: wiring flowers for bouquets and headdresses is a specialist skill and requires training.

Above left: An exotic Eastern display combines dendrobium orchids with bright red roses.

Right: A miniature garland for decorating the winter interior features the intense shades of anemones, set off with roses, moss and ivy leaves.

Above: An exercise in coordination: orange lilies, euphorbia and catkins with a vivid bowl of clementines.

CUTTING AND CONDITIONING

Most flowers will need to be trimmed once you have arrived home. The area of the stem presented to the water should be fresh – stem ends which have been out of water for any length of time tend to dry up and absorb water less efficiently.

It is a good idea to trim at least ½-1 inch (1-2 cm) from the stems, more if the arrangement requires. Cut the stems at an oblique angle so that the largest surface area possible is available to take up the water.

Once the stems have been trimmed, put the flowers into a deep bucket of water for two hours so a reservoir can be taken up into the heads. This is especially important if the flowers will be used long-stemmed. The same advice applies equally to flowers cut from the garden or pot plants.

SPECIAL CARE

Woody stems

The stems of certain flowers such as chrysanthemums, viburnum, cotoneaster and flowering foliages are fibrous and woody. To aid uptake of water, hammer the stems so they split and splinter.

Roses

Most roses come wrapped in plastic lining and the heads may have wilted or dropped slightly by the time you get them home. Remove the plastic lining and take off the thorns from the stems so that the flowers are more comfortable to work with. Trim the stems (they do not need to be hammered) and dip them into 2 inches (5 cm) of boiling water for 20 seconds to clear any airblocks. Then carefully wrap the flowers in tissue paper or newspaper and place in deep water for approximately two hours. Some of the foliage can be left on the stems to aid water absorption.

Euphorbia

Stems are sealed prior to sale. If you need to recut stems, they should be resealed by holding in a flame so that sap does not leak out.

Amaryllis

To prolong the life of cut amaryllis, turn the stem upside down and fill the hollow cavity with water, plugging with cottonwool.

Bulb flowers

Narcissi and hyacinths bleed a translucent sap when cut which can block stems. If you need to recut stems, trim under running water to wash the sap away.

WATER

Cool water will prolong the life of cut flowers. In some circumstances, however, you may wish to place the flowers in warm water to open buds and bring on the display ahead of time.

The water should be as deep as the container allows. The crucial relationship is between the length of the stem and depth of the water: the longer the stem, the deeper the water should be. Long-stemmed flowers in shallow containers will last a fraction of their normal lifespan.

Water is an alien medium for flowers; stems drown and decompose, depositing particles which change the chemical nature of the water. To slow down the process of decay, take off the foliage below the water line and change the water in containers as frequently as possible, retrimming the stems by ½ inch (1 cm) at each water change. You can also add a flower food to the water which will make the flowers last longer, but as this yellows the water it is best not used in see-through containers. With flower food, you can change the water every three to four days; without, allow only one or two days between changes.

One of the problems of needing to change the water frequently is that you run the risk of disturbing a carefully composed and balanced arrangement. If the flowers are all in good condition, you can stand the vase or container under the tap and leave the water running until it has come up over the side. But if some of the flowers are beginning to brown, changing the water provides an opportunity to discard dead and drying heads, retrim the stems of those which survive and rearrange, perhaps in a different container. In mixed arrangements, some species will last longer than others and so changing the water is a good way of gaining maximum value and enjoyment. Similarly, flowers in bud can be arranged in a tall, elegant container; once opened, they can be cut down and arranged in a lower vase to display the heads prominently.

Always clean containers thoroughly between use. Use bleach or a washing-up liquid and scour to remove the tidemark of algae and scum. Dirty containers only speed up the process of decay.

TEMPERATURE

In general, flowers do best positioned where they will not be subject to extremes of temperature.

Naturally warm places – near radiators, for example – will cause flowers to spoil quickly. You should also avoid placing flowers near working fireplaces and ovens. Very draughty locations such as hearths and doorways can also cause problems.

If you need to take flowers on a journey, pack them in a box so they do not get crushed and add a synthetic ice pack to keep them cool and fresh. The flowers should not touch the ice pack.

USING OASIS

Oasis or florist's foam consists of a green porous material, which is available in pyramid, square and cylindrical shapes as well as the standard blocks 12 × 6 × 4 in (30 × 15 × 10 cm). Although some people maintain that oasis promotes an artificial, contrived look, it can be used to create natural-looking arrangements and is extremely useful for deep or awkwardly-shaped containers. Oasis may also be the only means of creating certain shapes, such as those where flowers spill down over the edge of the container.

In some ways, oasis is a more "natural" medium for flowers than water. Oasis supports the stem in the same manner as earth or a branch. It holds a certain amount of water and presents it to the plant in the same way as earth: the flower draws as much water as it needs.

Despite these advantages, flowers generally do not last as long in oasis as they do in water.

The size and shape of the oasis will depend on the arrangement, container, and the quantity and size of stems. For a display where you want the flowers to flow down over the edge of the container, the block or blocks of oasis must stand far enough above the top of the container that stems can be inserted at an upward angle. Oasis is easy to cut; odd shapes can be built up by covering blocks with chicken wire. Chicken wire wrapped around oasis will also prevent it from crumbling excessively; this is especially advisable for large arrangements where many stems are being inserted. It may also be necessary to secure the oasis with waterproof tape.

After the oasis has been cut to size, it should be thoroughly soaked. Float the block on top of a sink or bucket of water. The oasis will become saturated in a matter of minutes. Do not push the oasis down to submerge it as this will cause air blocks and dry areas will remain inside.

Before you begin an arrangement, think about which direction you want the flowers to fall. Mentally divide the oasis in sections and insert the flowers in the relevant portion. Avoid crossing stems. A haphazard approach will create problems: the display will lack stability and the oasis will be more likely to break up.

Insert each stem by holding it low down and feeding it into the oasis. Do not try to insert the flower by pushing down from the head – the stem may buckle or even break. You need to insert at least 1½ or 2 inches (4-5 cm) of stem into the oasis so that the flower has a good chance of absorbing water. To insert thick stems it is often easier to make a hole first with a pointed tool to avoid damaging the stems.

The oasis should sit in a container filled with water. Top up the level daily, pouring water over the oasis as well as into the container. If the oasis is allowed to dry out, it is difficult to restore the necessary capillary action. Flower heads can be sprayed with a plant spray. Oasis cannot be reused, but it is cheap and widely available.

Below: A few arum lilies suggest the simplicity of the winter landscape combined with bare branches, foliage and fungi.

CHICKEN WIRE

Chicken wire is standard florist's equipment and has many varied uses. If a large arrangement needs to be transported, chicken wire wrapped around the oasis will prevent it from crumbling. Chicken wire also makes a good alternative to oasis for creating large displays. The wire should be crumpled and tangled so that the flowers remain stable.

Chicken wire also allows you to use a few flowers, or flowers with fine stems, in a wide-necked container. If the container is opaque, a ball of chicken wire pushed down inside will hold the flowers in place. For a glass container, you can lay a mesh of chicken wire over the neck and arrange the flowers within the grid. The wire can be easily disguised with moss placed on top of the grid. (Alternatively, you can construct the grid with plastic tape.)

WATER VIALS

Water vials, test tubes or "thimbles" are small glass containers of the type which are often seen enclosing the stems of orchids. They are available in about four sizes to suit different stems. The special advantage of vials is that they allow cut flowers to be combined with potted displays. The vial is inserted in the earth to hold water for the cut flowers, foliage or trails. The vial must be in an upright position and topped up daily with water. For a large arrangement, a small jam jar makes a cheap and readily available alternative.

WIRING

Wiring flowers consists of removing the stems and attaching lightweight wire to the flower head. The technique is mostly used for making wedding bouquets and headdresses, and for dried flower arrangements. Time-consuming, intricate, and demanding quite different skills from those used in flower arranging, wiring is best left to the professionals, especially for such important occasions as weddings.

Many people believe that wiring results in a stiff, unnatural-looking bouquet, but such rigid constructions are merely poor examples of the technique. It is perfectly possible to wire flowers so that they retain a sense of movement and fluidity. The great advantage of wiring is that it is possible to create trailing or curving shapes. And because the stems are removed, bouquets are considerably lighter and more comfortable to carry and headdresses are easier to wear for long periods. Wiring also helps avoid the flowers from becoming battered and gives extra support when they begin to wilt towards the end of the day.

The wire must be strong enough to support the flower, but not rigid. There are over twenty gauges of wire, from fine silver for wiring tiny hyacinth bells to heavier steel for attaching large carnation heads. In a bouquet, individual wires are drawn together and taped to make a comfortable handle. Special florist's tape is used which bonds together in the warmth of the hand.

The florist will be able to advise as to which flowers are suitable for wired bouquets or headdresses. The loss of stem inevitably shortens the life of flowers and certain species, such as anemones and snowdrops will not survive for long periods once the stems are removed.

Right: A matching door wreath and garland tieback consist of pine, cupressus, ivy, cones, walnuts and red chrysanthemums wired in place.

DRIED FLOWERS

Ten years or so ago, a dried flower arrangement too often meant a dusty, neglected display of luridly dyed grasses, together with a few helichrysums and statice, all looking rather more fake than dried. But like other areas of floristry, dried flower design has changed immensely; now, there is an incredible variety of dried flowers available, with new methods used to produce them.

Dried flowers will never look like fresh flowers and should never be treated as some kind of substitute for them. They are simply different; they provide different textures, different shades and different effects from the fresh flower range. In general, colours are more muted, petals are papery and more delicate and stems are frailer – ie what you would expect from moisture loss.

Commercial dried flowers are produced by kiln or freeze drying, both of which are rapid processes designed to retain as much of the original colour as possible. (The quicker a flower dries, the deeper and stronger its colour.) However, there are many types of flower which are easy to dry at home, an excellent way of prolonging your enjoyment of your summer garden. Most of these have fine stems: fleshy stems are slower to dry and there is consequently more chance of the flower rotting before it has been dried successfully.

FLOWERS SUITABLE FOR HOME DRYING

Achillea	Heather (impossible to fail)
Alchemilla mollis	Helichrysum (impossible to fail)
Amaranthus	Hydrangea
Anemone	Larkspur
Celosia	Lavender (impossible to fail)
Cornflower	Peony
Cynara	Protea
Delphinium	Ranunculus
Echinops (impossible to fail)	Rose
Gypsophila	Statice (impossible to fail)

Beech and magnolia leaves both dry well, as do artichokes and wheat. The seedheads of honesty, nigella and poppy can also be dried.

Right: Dried headdresses have a nostalgic appeal. These full, heavy circlets show that dried flowers need not be lacking in colour. Contents include lavender, larkspur, roses, hydrangea and amaranthus.

DRYING METHODS

All of the flowers on the preceding list, except for hydrangeas, are best dried by hanging from the stem down in a warm place such as an airing cupboard. A greenhouse may also be a suitable location, provided the atmosphere is not steamy.

The first step is to strip the foliage from the stems, as this contains excess moisture which will only slow down the process. Then tie the flowers in small bunches to allow the air to circulate and hang them upside down. Hanging will produce straight stems – if flowers are left standing in a vase, their necks will droop. Flowers such as roses should be picked as the buds are opening but before the flower is in full bloom. Hold the partially closed head over the steam from a kettle for 20 seconds; blow hard into the centre of the flower once it has dried if you want an open flower.

Hydrangeas dry better if they are left in a vase with two to three inches (5-7.5cm) of water. Once the water has been drunk, the flower gradually dries out. If hydrangeas are hung, they tend to shrivel. Hydrangeas, as well as gypsophila, magnolia leaves, beech and alchemilla, also benefit from glycerining. Add glycerine oil to two to three inches (5-7.5cm) of water in the ratio of one to three, and leave the flowers to stand. The glycerine will be absorbed by the flowers and keep the petals flexible and soft.

An alternative drying method is to use silica gel. But because so many crystals are needed, this technique is really only practical for drying a small amount of flowers. You can use silica gel to dry wedding bouquets; even freesia and gardenia can be dried in this way. The whole bouquet should be buried in the crystals.

To preserve the glossy appearance of nuts such as chestnuts or to protect foodstuffs such as pasta, apply a coat of clear wood varnish.

WORKING WITH DRIED FLOWERS

Most dried flowers are fairly frail and stems may not be able to support the heads which are liable to fall off. If this is the case, stems can be replaced by wire, with the

Right: Twists of green broom and dried vines, together with preserved magnolia leaves and cones make a dramatic decoration for the base of the candelabra.

wire being inserted in the flower heads for a secure result.

Alternatively, a mass of heads can be bound with steel wire, leaving stems intact. The technique involves making a wire stand known as a "double leg mount" which is used to hold the cluster of flowers together and insert it into moss or oasis.

Choose the gauge of wire depending on the weight of flowers. Bend one-third of the wire down and lay it onto the stems several inches above their base. Then wind the longer end several times tightly around the stems so that it finishes parallel with the first side. The two sides of the wire now facing down – the "double leg" – can then be used like a stand to hold the flowers in position.

Dried flowers are best arranged in a special type of oasis, which is harder and less crumbly than fresh flower oasis. (Dried flowers cannot be used together in wet oasis with fresh flowers because they will become mouldy.) Similarly, make sure that moss is quite dry if you are wiring dried flowers on to it.

Index

Numbers in italics refer to photographs

achilea, 106
Alchemilla mollis, 106; drying, 106
alstroemeria (Peruvian lily; *Alstroemeria* hybrid), 12, 21, 44, 57; pink, *32*
amaranthus, *77*, 86, 106, *107*
amaryllis (*Hippeastrum* hybrids), 12, *23*, 57; care of, 101
anemones, *27*, *56*, 57, *63*, 68, *73*, *99*, 106; red, *60*; white, *62*
apples, 30, 40, *74*; branches, 28
arrangement, types of 22, 28-31; at reception, 62; combining, 30; traditional Christmas and New Year, 22
artichokes, drying, 106
arums, *10*, *103*; yellow, *32*, 44, 48
attendants' flowers, 58-61
azalea (*Rhododendron simsii*), 12

baskets, 26, 28, 30; filled with dried flowers, 61; filled with gifts and flowers, 78
beech, drying, 106, 108
berries, 8, 30, 31
birch twigs, 46
botrytis, 8
bouquets, 56, *59*; bride's, 58; children's, 61; dried flower, 56; drying, 108; wiring, 104
bouvardia (*Bouvardia* spp.), 12
box (*Buxus sempervirens*), 12, 21
branches, 92; fir, 8; using, 22, 28
bride's flowers, 58
broom, green, *31*, *109*
brulia, grey, 48
bulbs, 8; care of flowers, 101

camellia, 34; leaves, *10*
Candlelit Table, 82-3
carnation (*Dianthus* sp.), 13, 21, 57, *73*
castor oil plant, foliage from, 44, 48
catkins, 44, *62*, *100*

celosia, 106
Ceramic Collection, 48-9
chestnuts, 8; varnishing, 108
chicken wire, 104
Christmas Eve, 94-5
Christmas Garland, 42-3
Christmas Pedestal, 68-9
Christmas rose (*Helleborus niger*), 13
Christmas Swag, 86-7
Christmas traditions, 75
Christmas tree: aromatic, 76; decorations, 75-6; edible, 76; folk art, 76; toy, 76
chrysanthemum (*Chrysanthemum* hybrids), 14, 21, 30, 57; care of, 100; red, 68, *105*
Classic Door Wreath, 84-5
cineraria, 62, 68
cinnamon sticks, 30, 76, *79*
circlets, *60*; bride's, 58; dried flower, *54*, *107*
clementines, *100*
colour, 25-6
Colour Accent, 44-5
combining arrangements, 30
conditioning, 100
cones, 8, *29*, 30, 50, 58, *59*, *72*, *74*, 76, 82, 90, 96, *105*, *109*; large, 86; small gold painted, 86; tipped with white paint, 88
conifer branches, 80
containers, 26-8; cleaning, 102; weddings, 62
Cool Whites, 34-5
Cornflower, 106
cotoneaster, care of, 100
Country Garland, 52-3
crocus (*Crocus* hybrids), 14, *24*
crystals, 56
cupressus (True cupress; *Cupressus glabra*), 14, 21, *59*, *60*, 90, 94, *105*
cutting, 100
cynara, 106

delphinium, 106
dill, white, *55*
dogwood, 28
Double Rose Buttonhole, 70-1
dried flowers, 30, 106; bouquets, 56, 58; home drying, 106, 108; pink, 42; suitable flowers for home drying, 106; wiring, 108-9; working with, 22, 108-9
driftwood, 50, 82, 88
drying methods, 108

echinops, 106
elaeagnus (*Elaeagnus* spp.), 14, 57, *59*
eucalyptus (*Eucalyptus gunnii*), *10*, 14, 21, *56*, 57
euonymus (*Euonymus* sp.), 14
euphorbia (Spurge; *Euphorbia fulgens*), 14, 57, 100; care of, 100; orange, 44, *63*

fir, 8
fir trees, 76
flower food, 101
foliage, 61
freesia (*Freesia* hybrids), 15, 21, 57; drying, 108
front doors, 26
fruit, 31, 64, 90
Fruit Bowl, 90-1
fungi, *62*, *103*

gardenia, drying, 108
gardens, flowers from, 11
garlands, 22, 61, *74*, *99*; at Christmas, 76; bride's, 58; in church, 62; preserved, *77*; tieback, *105*
Gelder rose, 32, 34
gifts, 78
gladiolus (Sword lily; *Gladiolus* hybrids), 16, 21, 57
glass cylinders, 26, 28
gypsophila, 21, 106; drying, 108

hanging decorations, *62*
hawthorn, *29*; twigs, 82
headdresses, dried, *107*; bride's, 58; wiring, 104
heather (*Erica* sp.), 16, *22*, 40, 57, *59*, 106
Hedera helix arborescens, 48
helichrysum, 106
helleborus, 57, 58
Heraldic Device, 80-1
holly (*Ilex aquifolium*), 8, 16, *23*, *55*, 57, 58, 64, *72*, *74*, 75, 88, 90, 94
honeysuckle, 11
hyacinth (*Hyacinthus orientalis* hybrids), 16, 57, 75
hydrangea, dried, 52, 106, *107*, 108

iris, 21
ivy (*Hedera* spp.), 8, *9*, *10*, 16, 21, *23*, 34, 36, 50, *55*, 57, *59*, *60*, 61, 64, 66, 70, *73*, 75, 82, *99*; flowering, 48; green, 88; variegated, 88

jam jars, 26
jasmine, 61
jugs, 26

kumquats, 30, *79*

lachenalia (spp.), 16
larch (*Larix* sp.), 16
larkspur, dried, 38, *54*, 106, *107*
laurel (*Laurus nobilis*), 16, 21, 40, *73*, 80, 88, 90
lavender, 52, 106, *107*; purple, 42
lichen, 8, *10*, 16, *23*, *28*, 82; covered branches, 88; dried green, 86; grey, 42; on hawthorn, 82; red, *73*
lily (*Lilium* spp.), 16, 21, 57; orange, 44, *100*; Longiflorum, 34; see also arum

magnolia (*Magnolia* spp.), 17; leaves, preserved, *73, 77, 84, 86, 109*; leaves, drying, 106, 108

Midwinter Colour 32-3

mildew, 8

mistletoe (*Viscum* sp., *Phoradendron* sp.), 17, 57, 58, 75

moss, 8, *9, 17, 21, 22, 28, 29, 30, 36, 42, 46, 68, 74, 82, 84, 88, 90, 99*; bun, *79, 92, 96*; sphagnum, *79, 86, 92, 96*; use of, 28

muffs, weddings, 61

muslin bags, 76

napkins, decorated, 78

narcissus (*Narcissus* hybrids), 17

nigella seedheads, *54*

nuts, 30, 31, *50, 64, 79, 90*

oasis, containers, 26; cuttings, 103; for dried flowers, 109; prevent crumbling, 103, 104; using, 102-3

orchid (*Dendrobium* sp.), 18, 21, 57; dendrobium, *98*

Party decorations and table settings, 76-8

pedestal arrangement, *63*

peony, 106; dried, 38

Pew End Decoration, 66-7

pine (Blue pine; *Pinus* sp.), 18, *54, 57, 59, 66, 73, 74*, 80, 88, 90, *94, 105*; base, *74*; blue, *60, 72*, 82

Pink Basket, 38-9

poinsettia (*Euphorbia polychroma*), 21, 75

poppies, *27, 63*; dried heads, *73*, 82

posies, 22, *55, 56, 61*; bride's, *58*; Snowdrop Posy, 64-5

pot pourri, 61, 96

Pot Pourri Basket, 96-7

protea, 106

potted plants, 62

ranunculus (*Ranunculus asiaticus*), 18, *23*, 57, 106

rose (*Rosa* hybrids), 18, *9, 10, 21, 57, 58, 59, 99*, 106; care of, 100; dried, 38, *54, 79, 107*; dried petals, 61; drying, 108; leaves, *54*; miniature spray, 42;

miniature, red, 58; red, *98*; spray, 52; white, *55*, 70

ruscus, 21

safety, 25-6

salix (White willow; *Salix alba*), 21

selecting flowers, 8-10

silica gel, 56, 108

silk flowers, 30

skimmia, *56*

snowdrop (*Galanthus nivalis*), 21, 28, 36, 57, 64

Snowdrop Posy 64-5

Snowdrops, 36-7

solidago, 32, 44, 48

special care, 100-1

star-anise, 30, 76

statice, 106

Study in Texture, 50-1

swag, *74*

temperature, 102

topiary, *79*

Topiary Trees, 92-3

tulips, 40

twigs, 8, 70; using, 22, 28

types of arrangement, 28-31

viburnum (*Viburnum tinus*), 21, 32, 34, *55*; care of, 100

vines, dried, *109*

violets, *24*, 40

Vivid Still Life, 40-1

water, 101-2; changing, 104

water vials, 104

wax flowers, *55*

weddings, 54; choosing flowers, 56-7; dresses, 58; flowers for the ceremony and reception, 61-2; pedestal arrangement, 63; registry office, 56; winter, 58

wheat, drying, 106

wheatsheaves, 30

willow twigs, 28, 30

winter cabbage, 40

Winter Greenery, 88-9

Winter Tree, 46-7

Winter Weddings, 54-5

wiring, 104-5; dried flowers, 108-9

woody stems, care of, 100

wreaths, 22, *29, 31, 72, 105*; at Christmas, 76; in church, 62

Acknowledgements

With special thanks to Liz Wilhide, Di Lewis, Kirsty Craven, Hilary Guy, Paul Morgan and the wonderful team at Pavilion Books, who have made working on this book such fun.

To all who have allowed me to ransack their homes for 'the sake of art', and to everyone slaving away at 56 James Street; Lucinda, Tracey, Andrea, Mark, Sam and Claire, without whom this book would have been impossible.

To my parents, Maurice and Brenda, and my sister Jill for their never-ending support.

Finally, to Linda Smith for the "palette" illustrations, and to Gill Elsbury for the line illustrations.

Jane Packer

The Publishers gratefully acknowledge the following for providing locations for photography:

Mr and Mrs Charles Fry, Chaddington, Wiltshire
Lynne Frank, Charles Thomson, Shirley Dent; London
St Clement's Church, Leigh-on-Sea, Essex
The photograph on page 6 is by courtesy
of the *Sunday Express* magazine